FABER NEW POE·

IN THE SAME SERIES

Declan Ryan

FABER & FABER

First published in 2014
by Faber & Faber Ltd
Bloomsbury House
74–77 Great Russell Street
London WC1B 3DA

Typeset by Hamish Ironside
Printed in England by Abbeystar

ACKNOWLEDGEMENTS

My thanks to Malene Engelund, Robert Selby, Liz Berry,
André Naffis-Sahely, Parisa Ebrahimi, Kim Patrick, Marianne
Burton, Colin Falck and all at Thurlow Road; to Jo Shapcott
and Andrew Motion; to Martha Sprackland and Matthew Hollis;
to the editors of *Poetry London*, *Poetry Review*, *The Spectator*,
The Best British Poetry 2013 and *Silkworms Ink*, where some of
these poems have been published; and to my family and friends.

A CIP record for this book
is available from the British Library

ISBN 978-0-571-32123-0

2 4 6 8 10 9 7 5 3 1

Contents

When We Were Kings

whales swam in our rivers, stranded
and hours from death, or arriving
at it. They were lost, as we are, branded

with an exile's stamp. Neither thriving
nor heartsick yet, their eyes unable
to adjust to foreign light, striving

for home in a manñer their fable-
thirsty rescuers distrusted. Citizens
spoke over breakfast tables

about these lost monsters: impatient;
unsure why these whales
in particular were newsworthy, friends

all of a sudden to the sea-shy, hailed
as martyrs of a sort. The fact remained:
it was in our rivers they had failed.

Ethiopia Shall Stretch Forth Her Hands
The Seven Commandments of Joe Louis

Joe Louis, mid-clinch,
is lifting his opponent –
the six-foot-six 'Ambling Alp', Primo Carnera –
into the air.
In The Hague
Italian and Ethiopian officials
have come to the end of their first day
of arbitration talks.
Here, in the Yankee Stadium,
Carnera will sink to his knees
'slowly, like a great chimney that had been dynamited'.

For breakfast this morning, Carnera consumed
a quart of orange juice, two quarts of milk,
nineteen pieces of toast, fourteen eggs,
a loaf of bread and half a pound of Virginia ham.
If he took the *Washington Post*
he will have seen a cartoon showing himself and Louis in
    the ring.
The illustrated Louis cast a dreadlocked shadow;
his shadow wore a crown.

Louis will start throwing bombs in the sixth round
and knock the Italian down twice
before a right–left combination
ends the fight.
Louis will touch a glove to Carnera's lower back
after the bell, and return to his corner
without celebration.

Louis has been given seven commandments
by his new manager to ensure he progresses
towards a title shot unhampered
by comparisons to Jack Johnson.
He is never to have his picture taken with a white woman.
He is never to go to a nightclub alone.
There will be no soft fights.
There will be no fixed fights.
He will never gloat over a fallen opponent.
He will keep a 'dead pan' in front of the cameras.
He will live and fight clean.

In 1964, Martin Luther King, Jr. will write
'More than twenty-five years ago, one of the southern states
adopted a new method of capital punishment.
Poison gas supplanted the gallows.
In its earliest stages, a microphone was placed inside
the sealed death chamber so that scientific observers
might hear the words of the dying prisoner.
The first victim was a young Negro.
As the pellet dropped into the container,
and the gas curled upward,
through the microphone came these words:
"Save me, Joe Louis. Save me, Joe Louis. Save me, Joe Louis . . ."'

The Donkey

My mother kept that story near her,
to belittle my father's village;
told us often how the one donkey
they'd brought into the place hanged itself
in the barn, days after market.
He bore it. Only one day she told it,
he came to my room before bed,
explained the root of it,
how when he was my age
but harder, not doughy with leisure
but thin as rushes,
they'd bought that needed beast
and it failed;
somehow tangled its neck in its tether
and ended.
He found it still and big-eyed
like it had seen a creature-god crouched over it
with kindness in the hollow of their palm.
He still pitied it,
acting out the ass of its name in the night,
though he knew it could never have been any good,
but might through wise rutting have sired an animal
who'd take the hardness out of the day,
carry in its bones all the dormant glory
of that cheap, doomed Abraham
remembered only in spiteful jokes
and the absolute emptiness of a hayshed.

From Alun Lewis

There is nothing that can save today, darling,
you not being here. You MUST write.
It's impossible to breathe otherwise.
I'm only talking of the things I really NEED.
I'm so tired of travelling away from you.
I think of you all the bloody time. Do you mind?

This isn't an answer or a letter –
it's only a cup of coffee after lunch.
Many things I've been unable to remember
came to me last night.
You sitting like a babu at a desk
in the bowels of the G.P.O.
You standing in the quartier Latin corridor
of the Hotel Marina on Sunday afternoon
after the cinema saying 'Alright, pay the taxi. Let's stay.'

When I saw you on Saturday July 24th
you were the flash of a sword.
Now I'm hopelessly shut into the camp life again.
A soccer match, a disjointed conversation at dinner,
a visit to the reading room to see how things go:
oh and a longing beyond words.

There's a fat dove strutting across the lawn
by the bougainvillea.
I wish I could be strolling with you
looking at the rose moles all in stipple
in your little stream.
One way or another I make a lot of shadows where I go.

Don't worry over the hairs on my head.
May you not be tried harder than you can bear.
Let there be an again, New Year. Save us.

The Range

'God save all here.' That's what you scored
into the metal of your childhood range.
The house was ruined when I saw it, a bored
boy of six or seven, nagging for a change
of scene as soon as we got there. Twenty
years are gone; I've not been back
to the village, the house, not for lack
of chances. Life is away, plenty
of it. You only asked that He save you. All.
You are dead, as is your mother.
Bad luck has clung to your brother
like an impermeable caul
he couldn't shake by getting out,
or having sons. He has one less. Since you.
For all the decay there was still the view
out back. Mountain family. Wiped out.

The blackbird is not a bad-luck bird.
The Blackbird of Avondale was not resigned
to arrears, in Kilmainham. He heard
a fresh start in letters Kitty signed
with kisses. He could not prevent Fiendish Park.
Later he could not prevent scandalising
a 'nonconformist conscience'; his larks
at Eltham almost vandalised
Home Rule. He had to go. 'If I go, I go forever.'
The 'hillside men' stayed loyal but the Master
couldn't have a mistress. Quicklime in his eyes, alive,
he sailed home for Hove and died. He was forty five.

III

You were betrayed; there is no other way
of saying this. The doctor told you to wash your hair
and go for walks; your appetite may
or may not return. He was only too aware
of your 'nerves' and said so.
He'd delivered all seven of your daughters
after all. They told you to go
back, anti-fatted calf, for more slaughtering
neglect. He rolled your dice for you for a season.
By the time he deigned to look for the real reason
behind your winnowing it was everywhere.
The doctor told you that you'd lose your hair.

IV

There is sadness in this blackbird's song,
and I know well what tuned it wrong.
It was those by whom the deed was done.
Now all its nestlings are gone.
This type of weather I also know,
and such a loss, not long ago.
I know it well, bird, I read your state
at the sight of a home left desolate.
It was sudden they came, the callous boys,
and quick the deed your young destroys.
You and I share a fate we both deplore.
My children, like your children, are no more.

V

When she turned thirteen your youngest child
was plagued by neighbours seeking cures.
The seventh girl of seven girls, a wild
sort of medic, they believed, the surest

route to remedy. You did not last
to see her giving birth. A boy,
out of a house of women. The past
will find him, eventually: its joys
and scandals. He will learn about you
from her; you will be photographs
and stories. She may spare him the true
ending and choose parts to make him laugh,
like your fierce temper, the black curtain
you pinned up to con the girls to bed
with the sun still high. Or, instead
she'll draw your life with a certain
pathos. You at seventeen, lovesick,
walking out 'to see Hughie Langan's duck',
when Hughie wasn't in, or sneaking Mick,
your stepdad, cigarettes 'for the road, and one for luck'.

VI

I found this in a book in a city you never visited:

A Charm Against Sorrow

This is a charm said by Mary for her son,
before the fair man and the turbulent woman
had laid him in the grave.
A charm that God set for himself, when the divinity
within him was darkened.
A charm to be said by the cross, when the night is black
and the soul is heavy with sorrow.
A charm to be said at sunrise, the hands on the breast,
when the eyes are red with weeping
and the madness of grief is strong.
A charm that has no words, only the silent prayer.

My mother called to say you'd gone.
I answered. She couldn't speak;
only made animal noise, a weak
throat sound which meant 'it's done'.

VII

In your dying days your daughters were visited by birds.
They stood in gardens, or entered their homes.
There were robins, for death, and blackbirds.
They are for resignation. You died at home,
light as a bird, bald as a young, blind bird.
Your children had all left but came back
to stay the night. Like your childhood
house on the hill, that home stands idle, its black
range unused also. Since you died there has been good
and bad news. More bad, I think, than good. A lot
of other leaving; the whole country is leaving, I'm told.
I could not live where the young leave before the old.
'God save all here', you wrote. You didn't say from what.

The Exaltation of Saint John Coltrane

He locked the door.
For five days straight he clucked;
an upper room,
skin pricked by poison thorns.
Cool gone west:
without his horn who knows what notes he heard;
an unsteady doo-wop of Philadelphia juncos,
the scat of leaves ecstatic after winter,
or a movement on the surface of the water
sipped between his shaky cigarettes?

He sought the Lord of Melody in silence,
pledged if he got his music back he'd preach
the Word, blow glossolalia
to make stones cakewalk in their beds,
beatify the redbricks of the Bronx,
bend every knee in prayer who ever laid
beside a stranger's mouth in smoky dark,
used lips to fix their solitary blues.

He heard a voice,
retreated for dictation to begin,
took down a hard-bop Torah in Dix Hills,
sent a coda of elation back to God,
placed his consecrated mouthpiece on his tongue
and blew.

'Girl in Bed'

New York cab, 12 September 1977

He brought the painting to be valued,
knowing something of the price
of this tantalising neck,
of the net that white bedsheets
made before he met this stare,
hard to believe in time before
he met this stare.

Brown paper bound gold hair,
which anyway fell
over a wrist;
wide blue eyes
the size of a husband's closed red fist.

He couldn't scrape together wealth to throw off
age, only a few flashy coins to pay for death,
his fellow passenger,
who opened the taxi door at Kennedy
and stepped inside;
ingredient of the Lowell blood at sixty years,
fisherman-elect at West 67th Street.

He wrapped up and carried the best woman in the world.
She was propped against him,
staring at nothing
as the meter stopped,
bulge eyes covered like the magician's stooge
who pretends not to see,
beyond a tied blindfold,
a man choose to disappear.

Transmission

I'm in my room, listening to your voice.
When this was live
you were in front of me, on stage,
in a red dress with a triangle cut in the back,
exactly the right size for my hand.

It wasn't long ago,
but the musicians must be somewhere else too,
their instruments boxed up,
waiting to go on in some new town.
They're running through it all again
here though; still nothing we can dance to.
Can you hear them where you are?

I suppose that was a sort of dance
on the platform, afterwards:
our feet shuffling towards one another's,
your palm on my chest,
exactly the right size for my heart.

My hand was at your spine then,
wondering if the shape cut in the fabric
was part of a wider unseaming,
or something I might have done to you
with my complicating touches.

If I'm remembering this correctly
you'd be met by applause
if you walked in right now,
asking to be completely undone.

Postcard from Australia

Cockatoos and rainbow lorikeets
are loudly showing off to one another,
high in the eucalyptus trees
that tower over this hinterland,
gorgeous in 7 a.m. light. No one's up.
You're lagging behind, still on last night,
asleep, no doubt, in that soft black T-shirt
whose logo gave up years ago; long before me.
Imagine how sunny it would be if you were here.

We've tried time-travel before, in those letters
we used to write, but this is something else.
Given the trouble I'm having
finding anything like a post office
I might see you before you read this,
or even be there when you do,
not daring to meet your eyes.

When you wake up for your big event
I'll already be sitting down to dinner in mosquito spray,
under a ceiling of abuse from the local geckos.
Even if I said 'to hell with this', and rushed off
to be with you, it'd be too late
and they'd have packed up the chairs before I arrived.
When I get home will you read to me
in your new orange dress,
and lie that it's for the first time?

Your last message came through in the small hours.
It looks like we'll have to go on missing each other,
trying to hit on a half hour of the day

when we're both awake.
I'll keep wondering before bed
why we aren't together,
then pretend I understand the new rules.

I can't wait until Tuesday means the same
for both of us again:
that place with the metal teapots,
your jumper pulled down over your hands,
your never staying for quite the full hour.

It'll be such a relief to have the present tense back,
having spent all these days in the past, or future, or both.
Whichever tense I'm in, I'm with you, little bee,
who are somehow outside of them all –
more exotic than any of their helplessly protesting creatures.
Whatever else, I want you to know that.

Trinity Hospital

There was a gunboat on the river
when you led me to your new favourite spot:
a home for retired sailors;
squat, white, stuccoed,
with a golden bell.

It could have been a lost Greek chapel,
a monument to light,
designed to remind the old boys
of their leave on Ionic shores
among tobacco and fruit trees.

Just after rain,
sunlight stood between us
like a whitewashed wall.
You were lit skin, gilt
and honey, dressed in olive.

No paper trail connects us.
No procedure of law
would tell you where to stand
in your sleek black mourning dress
if I die

but as you turned towards me
the golden bell rang to recognise
that I, being of sound mind,
will be delivered through orange groves
to you, the white church of my days.

Notes

'Ethiopia Shall Stretch Forth Her Hands' uses material from *Why Can't We Wait* (New American Library, 1964).

'From Alun Lewis' uses material from Alun Lewis's letters to Freda Aykroyd, collected in *A Cypress Walk* (Enitharmon, 2006).

Part IV of 'The Range' is a version of the twelfth-century Irish poem 'Cumhthach Labhras an Lonsa' ('It Is Sadly the Blackbird Calls').